IMAGES
of America

WORCESTER
VOLUME II

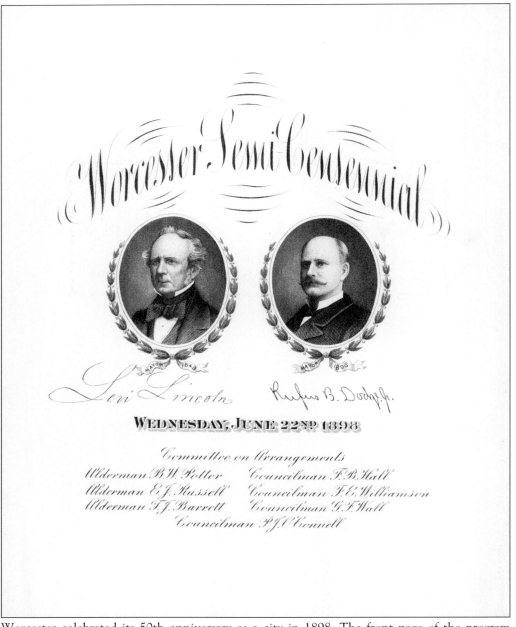

Worcester celebrated its 50th anniversary as a city in 1898. The front page of the program showed the city's first mayor, Levi Lincoln, and the then-current mayor, Rufus B. Dodge Jr.

IMAGES of America

WORCESTER
VOLUME II

Barton Kamp

ARCADIA

First published 1998
Copyright © Barton Kamp, 1998

ISBN 0-7524-0980-8

Published by Arcadia Publishing,
an imprint of the Chalford Publishing Corporation,
2 Cumberland Street, Charleston, South Carolina 29401.
Printed in Great Britain

Library of Congress Cataloging-in-Publication Data applied for

Dedicated to the memory of Harriet N. Kamp

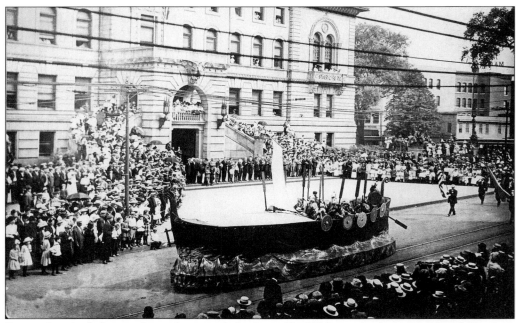

Over a hundred thousand people viewed the June 22, 1912 parade that was part of the city's
Swedish Midsummer Festival. One of the floats was of the *Anno*, a re-creation of the longboat
on which Lief Ericson sailed to America.

Contents

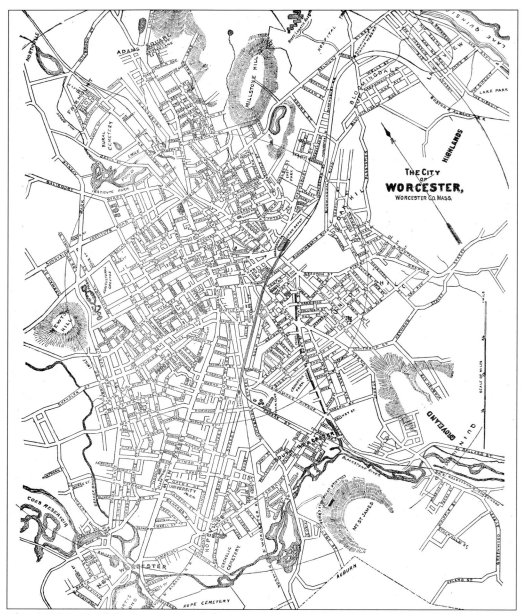

This 1898 map of the main part of the city was included in the *Pocket Guide to the City of Worcester*, published by George D. Monk.

Introduction

At the turn of the century Worcester was undergoing tremendous growth. Fortunately for us, it was at this time that the Golden Age of Postcards was in its infancy, because it is primarily through postcards that this growth was documented. The postcard craze had overtaken Europe by 1902 and by 1905 it had reached the United States in comparable proportions. In 1913 the United States, with a population of over 92 million people, recorded over 968 million postcards mailed. With Worcester's population over 160,000, it can be estimated that nearly 2 million postcards were mailed that year from the city.

The postcards were saved by the millions by placing them in albums, some of which held up to a thousand postcards. They were the cheapest and sometimes the only means of communication between businesses, friends, and families. Anyone with a camera could make a postcard. However, the majority of the postcards manufactured for the United States and the world came from Germany. The Germans had perfected the process to produce quality postcards. Prior to World War I the interest in postcards collecting began to diminish. The German companies that produced most of the world's postcards were destroyed during the war and their processes for producing postcards were lost. Changes in lifestyles after the war (i.e., more cars and telephones) reduced the need for and interest in postcards. Millions of postcards went into closets and attics to await the second postcard craze of the 20th century.

The growth of Worcester during the postcard era is best described in a book written by Donald Tulloch in 1914: "Few cities can show such tremendous growth in population. It has placed 3,000 people to its population every year on an average for 30 years. In the last 15 years it has added 50,000 people within its gates. Ah hour's ride by train, and Worcester can come in touch with 3,000,000 people, and that fact is true of one other city in the United States—New York."

The city is described also in Tulloch's book as follows: "Worcester is a unique city. There isn't anything just like it in the Western Hemisphere. First and foremost it is supremely a manufacturing and railroad center, and it is also a city of homes. It is a city of mechanics whose languages represent the nationalities of the universe, yet it is renowned as a center of music, art, culture, refinement."

It is the preceding paragraph that guided me in the selection of my images and how they would be presented. I visualized what a family would see and do upon arriving and settling in the city c. 1910. They would first encounter the city's streets and transportation. They would search for a job in manufacturing, in wholesale or retail, or in the services. They would become familiar with the city's buildings. They would join the church of their choice. They would make use of area schools. They would attend some of the many events that occur in the city.

This is the second book about Worcester in the Images of America series. It was prepared with the intent that it be a companion to the first Worcester book. Nearly all of the images in this volume are picture postcards covering the period from 1905 to 1930, though non-postcard images extend the coverage back to about 1890. Care has been taken not to duplicate any of the images of the first book.

One

Streets and Transportation

Salem Square met Front Street at the northeast corner of the common. The trolley is entering Front Street from Salem Square. Front Street was the main road to Union Station from the center of the city. Several hotels were located on the street to serve people arriving by train. The Essex, the Langdon, the Montreal, the Nashua House, New Sherwood, Sterling, and Warren Hotels were there c. 1910.

Lower Front Street, c. 1915, was the location of the Majestic Theater as seen on the left. Note the three-ball symbol of the pawn shop on the right at the entrance of Libby Loan Company. The loan company was one of the many pawn shops located on the street. The tower of the old Union Station can be seen in the distance. The Stars and Stripes flies on top of the Warren Hotel.

This is the end of Front Street, c. 1902. Washington Square began on the other side of the railroad viaduct. Canal Street was on the right. The wooden building on the right was a boarding house, and the Cape Cod Fish Company was located just before the viaduct.

Large American elm trees lined Front Street along the common. One of the trees had a growth in the shape of an elephant, which protruded from the trunk. It drew the attention of many passersby and was photographed extensively.

South of Chandler Street, Main Street, c. 1910, was still residential. The Trinity Church, seen on the left, was located at the corner of Main and Chandler Streets. On the right, at the corner of Mower (Ionic) Avenue, was the First Baptist Church. Next to the church was the home of Frank A. Leland, longtime owner of a piano and music store.

Trolleys from Southbridge Street merge with the Main Street trolleys at the intersection of Main and Southbridge Streets. Horse-drawn vehicles were the main means of transportation in this *c*. 1910 scene. A hard-to-find car heads up Chatham Street on the left. The tall building on the corner of Chatham Street was the Knowles Building.

From my window last October

Site preparation has begun for the construction of the city's newest building, the Slater Building. This picture, taken in October of 1906, shows workers setting up the barriers that will guide the pedestrians around the construction site. The building was opened in 1907.

Court House Hill and Main Street. WORCESTER, Mass.

Not a car in sight as this gentleman attempts to jaywalk across North Main Street at Court House Hill in 1908. He's probably headed for the trolley barn or the Exchange Hotel on the corner next to it. The First Unitarian Church is visible on Court House Hill.

The traffic is light as it heads north from Lincoln Square in this *c.* 1920 scene of Salisbury Street. The Central Church is on the left at the corner of Institute Road. The State Armory is in the distance. The Whitcomb Envelope Company and the Hobbs Manufacturing Company were located along the right side of the street.

Three churches are visible in this 1910 scene of Pearl Street, looking west from Main Street. On the left is the Plymouth Church, located on the corner of Chestnut Street. In the center is the Chestnut Street Congregational Church, and the spire beyond that belongs to the Pleasant Street Baptist Church.

The trolley on the causeway that crosses Lake Quinsigamond is headed toward Shrewsbury. The two sides were originally connected by a floating bridge. On January 20, 1905, a bill was introduced in the state legislature to build a bridge over the lake to replace the causeway. The bridge was to cost $125,000 and be 30 feet above the water. When the bridge was finally completed in 1919 its total cost came to $325,000.

Russell Street, shown here in winter, extends from Queen Street, past Elm Park, to Institute Road. The portion of the street near the park was formally called Agricultural Street. The street was named after James W. Russell, who owned a greenhouse on Pleasant Street in 1842.

Merrick Street, shown here in winter, runs from Cedar Street, across Pleasant Street, and up to Austin Street. Hitching posts line the street like parking meters. Merrick Street was named after the family name of Mrs. D. Waldo Lincoln, wife of the former mayor of Worcester.

Florence Street is located off May Street near Park Avenue. It extends from May to Beaver Street. The east side of Florence Street runs along the campus of Clark University. The double- and triple-decker apartment buildings provided housing for many of the students of the university.

Fales Street is located in the Greendale section of the city. The street extends from West Boylston Street to Burncoat Street. The residents of the street worked at the many manufacturing companies, including the Norton Company and Bradley Car Works, which were located in this part of the city.

Austin Street, located near Queen Street, is pictured here in the winter months, *c.* 1910. Austin Street extends from Main Street to Dewey Street. It is named after Rev. Samuel Austin, the fourth permanent pastor of Old South Church.

A lone horse-drawn sleigh travels down Hollywood Street in winter. Note the clear sidewalks and the snow-covered road. The main mode of transportation was the horse-drawn sleigh in 1910, so the streets were kept snow-covered for easy movement.

"WORCESTER, CITY OF PROSPERITY"

This is a view of Washington Square, *c.* 1912. The lower end of Front Street can be seen beyond the railroad viaduct. On the left is the new Union Station. On the right are the Washington Square Pharmacy and the Central Vermont Railway Agency.

Salem Square was located at the east end of the common. It extended from Franklin Street to Front Street. The two churches, shown here in 1907, were the Swedish Congregational and the Notre Dame Churches. The Notre Dame Church was located on Franklin Street until it was destroyed by fire.

Vernon Square, now known as Kelly Square, doesn't look very busy here, *c.* 1910. Vernon Street is on the left and Millbury Street is on the right. Water and Green Streets also enter the square. The Hotel Vernon is at the corner of Vernon and Millbury Streets.

Newton Square

The trolley enters Newton Square from June Street. Pleasant Street enters the square from the left, exits the square, and heads northwest. Highland Street enters the square on the right. The public tennis courts are in the foreground.

The Boston and Albany train passes through the Bloomingdale Cut on its way to Boston. The area around Plantation Street that runs from the fire station to Belmont Street was known as Bloomingdale. The cut can be seen from the bridge on Plantation Street that passes over the tracks.

Boston & Albany R. R. Restaurants

WORCESTER

Pittsfield   Springfield

MENU

Little Necks on half shell 20   Clam Cocktail 25

SOUPS

Clam Stew 30   Clam Bouillon 20   Chicken Broth with Rice 20
Tomato Soup 20   Consomme, hot or cold 15
Oyster Stew 30, with Cream 40

FISH

Broiled Fish 45   Broiled Live Lobster

RELISHES

Sliced Tomato 20
Gherkins 10   Queen Olives 15   Chow Chow 10

ROASTS

Roast Prime Ribs of Beef 60

STEAKS, CHOPS, ETC., FRIED OR GRILLED

Sirloin Steak 85   Tenderloin Steak 70   Porterhouse Steak $1.40
Small Steak 65   Broiled Lamb Chops (2) 50   Pork Chops 50
Broiled Chicken, half 70, whole $1.30
Hamburger Steak 40   Fried Chicken a la Maryland, half 75
Broiled Ham 40, with eggs 50   Broiled Bacon 40, with eggs 50
Roast Beef Hash with green peppers 40; dropped egg 50
Breaded Veal Cutlet, tomato sauce 50   Broiled Sausage 45
Welch Rarebit 35   Chicken Croquettes 40, with Green Peas 50
Minced Chicken with green peppers 50
Mushroom Sauce 30   Tomato Sauce 15   Smothered Onions 15

EGGS

Shirred Eggs (2) 20, (3) 30   Boiled (2) 20, (3) 30   Fried (2) 20, (3) 30
Scrambled (2) 20, (3) 30   Poached (2) on toast 25, (3) 35

OMELETS

Spanish 50   Plain 30   With Parsley 35   With Mushrooms 40
With Ham, Bacon, Tomatoes, Jelly, Cheese or Onions 35

VEGETABLES

Asparagus, Vinaigrette or drawn butter, (hot or cold) 30
Lima Beans 15   Corn 15   Succotash 15   String Beans 15
Domestic Peas 15   Tomatoes 15   Spinach 15, with egg 20

This is the second page of the menu of the Union Station Restaurant. The new station opened in 1911, after several delays. The restaurant was called the Boston & Albany Railroad Restaurant. The railroad also maintained restaurants at the stations in Springfield and Pittsfield.

22

POTATOES

Hashed Brown 15   French Fried 15   Hashed in cream 15   Saute 15
Lyonnaise 15   German Fried 15   Delmonico 20   O'Brien 20

COLD MEATS

Sardines, per order 25   Roast Chicken 65   Boiled Smoked Tongue 50
Boston Baked Beans 25   Boiled Ham 50   Roast Beef 50
Lobster boiled in shell   Corned Beef, Potato Salad 50
Pickled Lamb's Tongue 30

SALADS

Chicken 50   Potato 20   Lobster   Lettuce 25   Salmon Salad 40
Lettuce and tomato with French dressing 25

SANDWICHES

Tongue 15   Ham 10   Sardine 15   Chicken 20   Corn Beef 15
American Cheese Sandwich 10   Hot Roast Beef 30   Cold 20
Special Club Sandwich 35   Ham and Egg 25   Egg 15

GRIDDLE CAKES

Wheat Cakes with maple syrup 20

BREAD AND TOAST

French Bread 10   Home-made Bread 10   Bread with milk 15
Half and Half 25
Crackers with milk 15   Graham Crackers with milk 15   Dry Toast 10
Milk Toast 15   Buttered Toast 10   Cream Toast 25   Crullers 10
French Toast 35

DESSERT

Assorted Pies per cut 10   Ice Cream 15   Jelly Roll 10   Cup Cakes 10
Assorted Cake 10   Fruit Cake 10   Whole Grape Fruit 20
Cookies 10   Bananas with cream 20   Orange 10   Sliced Orange 15
Preserved Figs 20   Orange Marmalade 15
Pie a la Mode 20

American Cheese with crackers 15

Cup Coffee 10, pot 20   Small Pot Tea 10   Cup Cocoa 10   Instant Postum 10
Milk per glass 5   Horlicks Malted Milk 10

Tea Biscuits or Bread and Butter with all orders amounting to
fifty cents or over.

White Rock   bottle 25   Imp. Ginger Ale (C.&C.)   25
White Rock   splits 15   Clicquot Club, per bottle,   15
Domestic Ginger Ale, per glass,   10

Imported and Domestic Cigars

PLEASE PAY CASHIER

**An extra charge of ten cents will be made where two persons are served
from a single order.
No checks issued at table for less than twenty-five cents.**

G. W. ANDREWS, MANAGER.   J. H. MARCY, SUPT DINING SERVICE.
WORCESTER, MASS.   BOSTON, MASS

Page three of the menu lists lobster boiled in its shell. Like today's menus, it appears no price was printed for the lobster.

Car 167 of the Worcester Consolidated Street Railroad Company was a nine-bench, open car. The South Worcester Trolley, c. 1910, ran from Green Hill Park to Holy Cross College. The railway company was the oldest and largest railway system in the city. It was formed in 1887 by consolidating two horse-railway systems—the Citizens Street Railway Company and the Worcester Street Railway Company. In 1892 the company was granted the right to change from the slow-going, horse-car system to one of electric propulsion. By the end of 1893 all cars were run using electric power.

Two

Home

Exchange Hôtel, 93. Main Street, Worcester, Mass.

The Exchange Hotel, shown here c. 1906, was located at 93 Main Street, on the corner of Market Street. Known as the United States Arms Hotel at the end of the 18th century, this was the city's oldest hotel. George Washington stopped here for breakfast in 1789 while on his way to Boston. Lafayette was a guest at the hotel in 1825.

The Aurora, Worcester, Mass.

The Aurora Hotel was located at 656 Main Street, near Chandler Street. It was a select, high-grade, family hotel, with single rooms as well as suites. The rooms were either finished or unfinished, and there were special rates for prolonged stays.

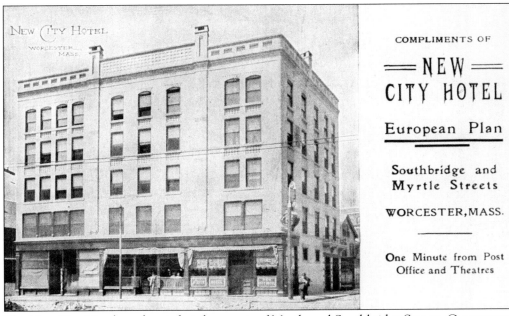

New City Hotel
WORCESTER, MASS.

COMPLIMENTS OF

=== NEW ===
CITY HOTEL

European Plan

Southbridge and Myrtle Streets

WORCESTER, MASS.

One Minute from Post Office and Theatres

The New City Hotel was located at the corner of Myrtle and Southbridge Streets. Constructed in 1891, it contained 35 bedrooms.

The Standish Hotel was located at 767 Main Street, at the corner of Jackson Street. In 1911 it offered accommodations for permanent and transient guests, with a first-class garage nearby.

The Bellmar Hotel was located at 667 Main Street, on the corner of Mower (Ionic) Avenue. It was one of the city's private hotels, formerly known as fashionable boarding houses. The number of boarding houses in the city increased from 50 in 1870 to about 80 in 1920. People who rented their rooms planned to stay longer than just a few days.

HOTEL DEVENS. 166 MAIN STREET. WORCESTER, MASS.

Decorated in honor of the end of World War I, Hotel Devens was located at 166 Main Street. This type of hotel, with stores on the street floor and rooms on the upper floors, catered to the visitors entering the city c. 1920. An average of ten thousand people entered the city daily, either by passenger train or by street railways. They preferred to stay in rooming or boarding houses, or private hotels, rather than lavish hotels like the Bancroft.

This large home was located at 1 Brooks Street in the Greendale section of Worcester. At the turn of the century this was the farmhouse of John A. Kendrick.

This large home is located at 155 Lincoln Street at the corner of Perkins Street. Around 1910, the house was occupied by a salesman, a nurse, an envelope maker, a wireworker, a lineman, and a carpenter.

This was the 1910 home of Ward M. Amsden at 36 Uxbridge Street. Uxbridge Street is located near Lincoln Street. Mr. Amsden was a watchmaker whose place of business was at 418 Main Street.

One of the many triple-deckers located in Worcester was located at 3 Shirley Street. That street is just off of Park Avenue. Around 1911, Walker Woodhead, a clerk at the Boston & Albany Freighthouse, lived on the first floor; William Gilbert, a repairer, lived on the second floor; and L. Gilbert Arnold, a bag maker, lived on the third floor.

The picture of this beautiful home at 23 Chestnut Street was taken about 1907. The owners of the home were Mr. and Mrs. John C. Dewey. Mr. Dewey was a prominent lawyer in the city.

This home is located at 6 Lisbon Street near Coes Reservoir. Around 1912 it was occupied by Mr. and Mrs. Herbert Fisher. Mr. Fisher was an inspector for the city.

This large home is located at 32 Westland Street, which is off Highland Street near Elm Park. The home was occupied in 1911 by Allan B. Miller, who was a clerk at Worcester Mechanics Savings Bank.

This picture of 523 Cambridge Street was taken in 1914. The house was located across the street from the Cambridge Street School, near Southbridge Street. In 1925 Harold Estabrook (a salesman), Joseph Westwood (a weaver), Earl T. Harper (president of Parker and Harper Mfg. Company), and Carl Hedberg (a packer), resided at the house.

This home is located at 22 Kingsbury Street at the corner of Queen Street. In 1912 the first floor was occupied by John T. Sheehan, a mailman; the third floor was occupied by Arthur T. Church, a foreman at the Worcester Machine Screw Company.

This is 299 Lincoln Street, at the corner of Shattuck Street, as it appeared in 1908. Located near Hahnemann Hospital, it was used as the home for over 20 graduate nurses.

BEAUTIFUL HOMES OF LENOX NEIGHBORS.

Everett J. Harrington

Harry C. Robinson

Otis W. Everett

Good Health

GETTING the family away from the small apartment and congested neighborhood with vitiated air and surrounding them with the clean, wholesome conditions which prevail at LENOX will inaugurate a new state of health and bodily vigor. The ideal home site for children is LENOX. The environment of clean surroundings and the companionship of refined boys and girls is a most important consideration in selecting a home.

You Say
Good Morning
Good Neighbors
LENOX

Edgar C. Fowler

William Hart

Albert L. Bemis

LENOX IS THE BEAUTY SPOT OF WORCESTER.

Lenox was a housing development on the city's west side, c. 1910. It encompassed both sides of Pleasant Street, beyond Richmond Avenue, and included the following streets: Lenox, South Lenox, Berwick, Beeching, and Chamberlain Parkway. Pictured at the top pf the page are the homes at 25 Beeching Street, 46 Beeching Street, and 9 Beeching Street; at the bottom of the page are the homes at 26 Lenox Street, 6 Lenox Street, and 22 Lenox Street.

The Beauty Spot of Worcester

T HE view and outlook from this ideal home site are superb. LENOX is being beautified and improved on the most liberal lines, without cost to present purchasers. Large lots, wide streets, built to grade accepted by City Engineer; parkways, a new feature in the development of home sites in this city; shade trees, water, gas, sewers and all city improvements. The natural charms of scenic beauty and delightful surroundings and our high-class development work, involving an actual expenditure of over $60,000 combine to make LENOX the beauty spot of Worcester.

You Say
Good Morning
GOOD NEIGHBORS
LENOX

James F. Estes   Marcellus Roper   Albert F. Richardson

LENOX IS THE BEAUTY SPOT OF WORCESTER.

The city's population grew from about 58,000 in 1880 to 180,000 in 1920. With that growth came the need for more housing. Lenox offered single-family homes to the professionals and well-to-do living in the city. Pictured here are the homes at 15 Berwick Street, 11 Kensington Road, and 879 Pleasant Street.

Worcester, Mass., Residence of M. J. Whittall.

Pictured *c.* 1910, the home of Matthew J. Whittall was located at 692 Southbridge Street at the corner of Cambridge Street. He was a manufacturer of carpets with a plant on Brussels Street in South Worcester.

Located at 921 Main Street was the home of William A. and Mary A. Richardson. Mr. Richardson was one of the founders of the Harrington and Richardson Arms Company. He died in 1897. Mrs. Richardson died in 1910.

Three
Manufacturers

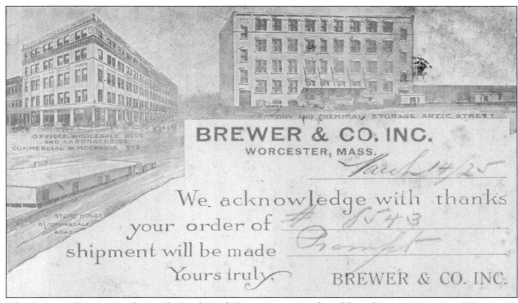

The Brewer Company, formerly Bush and Company, was the oldest drug company in Worcester County. It manufactured tablets and elixirs for physicians. Its offices, wholesale department, and laboratories were located on Mechanics and Commercial Streets, the factory and chemical storage building was located on Arctic Street, and the warehouse was located on Bloomingdale (Franklin) Road.

Bradley Car Works, Worcester, Mass.

The Osgood Bradley Car Works was located on West Mountain Street, near West Boylston Street, in Greendale. Formerly located at Washington Square, in 1909 it had to move to make way for the construction of the new Union Station. In 1914 the company employed over 1,600 men. It was capable of turning out six hundred all-steel railroad cars per year.

This is one of the products of the Osgood Bradley Car Company—a passenger car built for the New York, New Haven, and Hartford Railroad. In 1822 the company began by building carriages and state coaches. With the coming of the railroad, the company sold the carriage business and devoted its time to making railroad cars. The company also built trolleys and buses.

KINDLY SEND INFORMATION CONCERNING YOUR WRENCHES

The Coes Wrench Company, shown here on the left, was located at Coes Square. The Loring Coes Company, a division of Coes Wrench Company, was located at the corner of Mill and Coes Streets, on the shores of Coes Reservoir and Coes Pond. The Coes's residence is shown in the right foreground. Upon completion of the new city hall, the old town hall was torn down and the hall clock was placed in the clock tower of the residence.

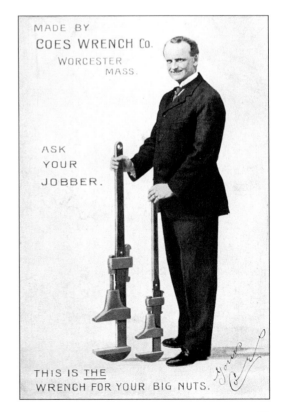

Mr. Coes shows off his wrenches. The key model Coes's screw wrench is the heaviest, strongest, largest-capacity screw wrench made. It comes in four sizes—28-inch, 36-inch, 48-inch, and 72-inch.

The Graton and Knight Manufacturing Company was located on Bloomingdale Road. The company tanned leather and manufactured belting from it. Manufacturing plants needed belting for the transmission of power.

The Harrington and Richardson Arms Company was located at Park Avenue and Chandler Streets. It manufactured revolvers and shotguns. The business was founded in 1871 by Gilbert H. Harrington, who took on William A. Richardson as a partner in 1874.

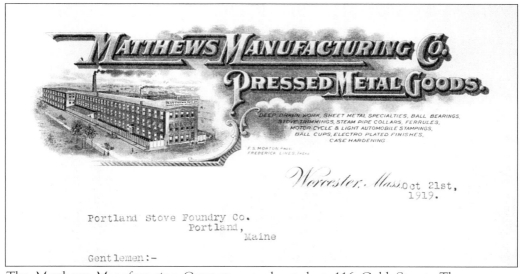

The Logan, Swift, and Brigham Envelope Company was located at 75 Grove Street. All of the machinery in the factory was invented and built by the Swifts. The company made envelopes in every conceivable size and shape.

The Matthews Manufacturing Company was located at 116 Gold Street. The company manufactured all kinds of furnishings for heating apparatus and light-weight, cold-rolled steel for the manufacture of bicycles.

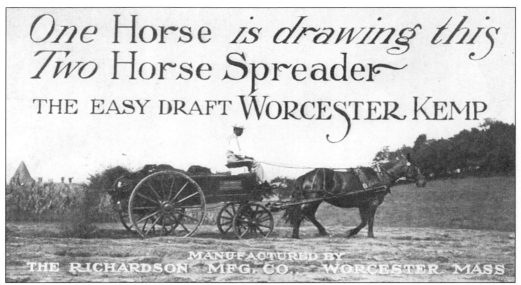

The Worcester Kemp Manure Spreader was one of the many products manufactured by the Richardson Manufacturing Company. The company, located at 84 Prescott Street, also manufactured the Worcester Buckeye Mower, the Bullard Hay Tedder, and the Worcester Horse Rake. In 1910 Edwin P. Curtis was president and John D. Curtis was vice-president of the company, which manufactured many kinds of agricultural implements.

Stephen M. Sargeant, president, and S. Mortimer Sargeant, treasurer, were the officers of the S.M. Sargeant Company in 1910. The company manufactured extracts and toiletries and its laboratories were located at 107 June Street.

Oilzum, a carbonless, gas-engine-cylinder oil, was manufactured by the White & Bagley Company, which had offices at 100 Foster Street and a factory on Manchester Street. The White & Bagley Company started business in 1889 in a small, frame building on Woodland Street with Herbert P. Bagley as president and Fred W. White as treasurer. The company was an extensive manufacturer of oils and greases for lubricating purposes.

J.J. Coffey, racecar driver, gives testimony to the benefits of Oilzum. He won the Dead Horse Hill climb on June 12, 1909. The Dead Horse Hill climb took place on Stafford Street for several years at the beginning of the 20th century. The race has been revived in recent years.

This quarry on Millstone Hill was located in part of Green Hill Park. The facility was operated by George B. Webb, a general contractor. The granite mined was used in buildings, monuments, curbing, and paving. George D. Webb died on December 28, 1910.

Pictured here is the George C. Whitney Company—the largest manufacturer of valentines in the world, c. 1910. It also manufactured postcards, art goods, and novelties. On January 12, 1910, starting at 9 p.m., the company's five-story factory at the corner of Union and School Streets was burned to the ground. On January 22, 1910, the company purchased buildings nearby on Union and School Streets and resumed manufacturing with little interruption, despite the recent fire.

The White, Peavey, and Dexter Company packed pork. Their factory, shown here, was located on Putnam Lane off of Shrewsbury Street.

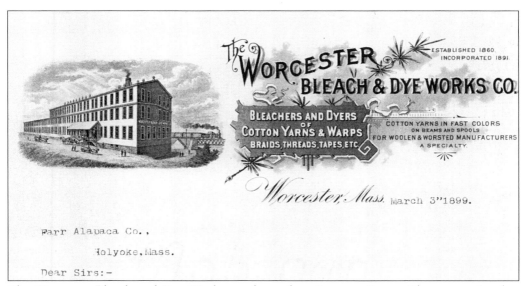

The Worcester Bleach and Dye Works was located on Fremont Street. The companies that manufactured fabrics in the city were the customers of this dyeing company—the leading company in the industry.

The Worcester Ferrule and Manufacturing Company, located at 17 Hermon Street, was the pioneer in the manufacture and sale of ventilated stove knobs. The company also manufactured steel and brass ferrules, bicycle bearing cases, and other specialties.

The office staff of the Wright Wire Company posed for this picture c. 1910. The company, located at 69 and 71 Hammond Street, manufactured copper, brass, galvanized, tinned, steel, and iron wire cloth. There were more wire manufacturers located in Worcester than any other city in the country at the turn of the century.

Four

Businesses

The H.A. Ballou Pain Store was located at 143 Main Street. The signs in the windows announce the availability of tickets to the envelope employees' excursion to Nantasket Beach and Plymouth Rock.

The Alsten and Goulding Company was located at 36 Foster Street. It was a wholesaler and retailer of rubber tires for automobiles, carriages, and bicycles. The site became known as "the rubber tire corner."

The Alsten and Goulding Bicycle and Buggy Repair Shop is shown here. A 1911 advertisement says that, "it is the largest vulcanizing plant in central New England."

BELL BROTHERS
CONFECTIONERY & ICE CREAM PARLORS
WORCESTER, MASS.

Bell Brothers Confectionery and Ice Cream Parlor opened at 152 Front Street before 1910. The Bell brothers also owned a store at 558 Main Street. The store at 152 Front Street was later occupied by the Union Loan Company, a pawn shop owned by the author's father prior to its demolition, which made way for the Worcester Center Galleria.

The Besse-Bryant Company was located at 24 Front Street. This store was one of 27 stores in the Besse System. The Besse System celebrated its 50th anniversary in 1927. The stores of the Besse System had the purchasing power of a chain store, but each one was operated as an individual store whose manager lived in the community in which it was located.

The general offices of Claflin-Sumner Coal Company were located at 9 Pleasant Street. Wholesalers and retailers of anthracite and bituminous coal, the company maintained yards on Southbridge and Shrewsbury Streets.

The Denholm and McKay Company, also called the Boston Store, was Worcester's largest department store. It was located across from city hall, opposite Franklin Street.

The new Slater Building contained an arcade of stores. This is the Beatrice Gloucester Candy Shop, located in the arcade. It carried everything in the line of confectioneries.

Jacob Holden and Antipas F. Earle celebrated ten years, from March 15, 1888, to March 15, 1898, in the cigar and tobacco business. Their shop was located at 434 1/2 Main Street.

The halftone engraving room of the Howard-Wesson Company was located on the fifth floor of the Day Building on Main Street in 1910. In 1921 it was located in the Graphic Arts Building located on the corner of Foster and Commercial Streets. The company printed catalogues, magazines, letterheads, cards, and announcements using the halftone process.

A.E. Hurd stands beside his horse and wagon. A resident of Charlotte Street, he sold his wares of teas, coffees, spices and extracts, butter, eggs, canned goods, and small groceries in the area around south Main Street.

George S. Kalashian poses in his delivery truck outside of his 147 Green Street Ice Cream and Confectionery Store, which manufactured velvet ice cream. A 1910 advertisement states, "Never hesitate to order by phone. No order too small for our attention; none too large for our facilities."

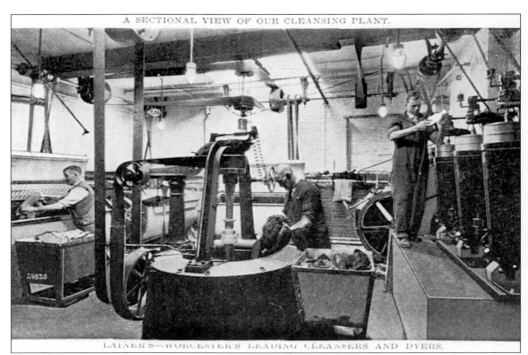

LAINER'S—WORCESTER'S LEADING CLEANSERS AND DYERS.

The cleansing plant of Lainer's, Worcester's largest cleaners and dyers, is shown here. Offices were located at 73 Green Street, and the factory was located on Plymouth Street.

Lasky's Worcester's Most Progressive Specialty Store, corner Main and Federal Streets, Worcester, Mass.

Everything a Woman or Miss Wears from Hosiery to Hats.

Laskey's was located on the corner of Federal and Main Streets. It was a retailer in women's apparel. In 1928 this location became a Filene's store.

John C. Mac Innes
Company,
Worcester,
Mass.

The John C. MacInnes Company was located at 454 Main Street across from city hall. It was a wholesale and retail dealer in dry goods, silks, draperies, cloaks, etc. The business was founded in 1873. By 1898 it had grown to encompass all four floors of three adjacent buildings.

The best Sanitary Shower Bath in New England. A trial will convince you.

Sanitary Shower Bath, Neptune Turkish Bath, 36 Church Street, Worcester, Mass.

Men prepare to take a shower at the sanitary shower bath of the Neptune Turkish Bath located at 36 Church Street. After taking a bath you were advised to use the swimming pool by a sign which read, "to avoid catching a cold you must take a good swim in the pool after the bath."

The interior of the Putnam and Thurston's Restaurant, shown here, was located at 381 Main Street in 1910. The restaurant later moved to 27 Mechanic Street. Founded in 1858, the restaurant was operated by Edward J. Putnam and Frank E. Thurston in the late 1800s.

Sharrott's Casino was located in the Lowell Building at the corner of Norwich Street and Foster Street. The casino was operated by Frank A. Sanderson.

This car, built for the W.H. Sawyer Lumber Company in the 1920s, was used to advertise the company in many parades. The office and lumberyards of the company were located at 66 Lincoln Street near Lincoln Square. William H. Sawyer served the city as alderman, as a member of the parks commission, and as chairman of the commission that directed the construction of the new city hall.

Samuel R. Small, operator of the "little grocery store" at 338 Pleasant Street, poses on his buck board. The store offered coffee, butter, flour, bundle wood, coke, charcoal, coal in bags, lard, canned goods, and fresh bread and milk for sale.

Delivery men pose with their wagons at Union Laundry c. 1910. The company, which kept 16 wagons and 21 horses employed in the collection and distribution of laundry, was located at the corner of Union and Exchange Streets. Founded in 1886 by David A. Scott, the company grew very rapidly. Mr. Scott originated the wet wash business in this country.

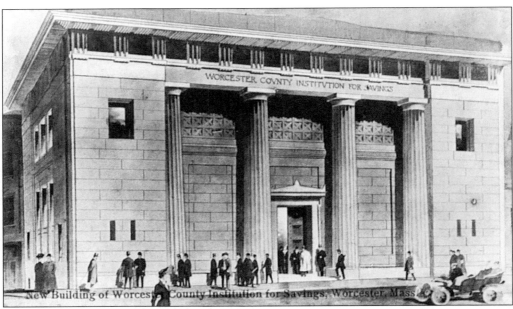

Worcester County Institution for Savings, the 11th savings bank chartered in the state, opened for business in its new quarters at the corner of Main and Foster Streets on October 29, 1906. The vault, three stories in height, was the largest bank vault in the city. The street-level floor was surrounded by 16 inches of cement and 3 inches of chilled steel. Equipped with various kinds of burglar-proof and alarm contrivances, the vault held the cash, securities, and valuable papers.

The ice man, with his wagon and team of horses, poses for this picture in front of a Main Street home. The owner of the wagon, Worcester Cold Storage Company, manufactured pure, artificially made ice from water furnished by their own, especially constructed, artesian well.

Shoppers are parked outside the Worcester Market at 621 Main Street near Madison Street. The rooms of the Hotel Kenmore were located above the market. The Dodge Furniture Store was located at 615 Main Street.

Worcester Telegram, Worcester, Mass.

WORCESTER TELEGRAM

The new Worcester Telegram Building was built on Park (Franklin) Street *c.* 1910. The *Worcester Sunday Telegram*, a Republican newspaper, was started in 1884 by Austin P. Christy. In 1886 the first *Worcester Daily Telegram* was published.

THE WORCESTER EVENING POST

A DAILY SCENE (OVER)

Carriers of the *Worcester Evening Post* pose in front of city hall *c.* 1920. The paper was started in 1891. It was the only Democratic daily in central Massachusetts at the time.

Five

Buildings

The American Antiquarian Society was founded by Isaiah Thomas in 1812. It was located at the corner of Highland Street and Court House Hill until the new building was constructed at the corner of Park Avenue and Salisbury Streets.

The Worcester Society of Antiquity was organized in 1875. In 1919 it changed its name to the Worcester Historical Society. Its purpose is "to foster in its members a love and admiration for antique research and archaeological science, and to rescue from oblivion such historical matter as would otherwise be lost."

The Worcester Armory, located at Grove and Salisbury Streets, was erected in 1889 and dedicated on January 30, 1891. Prior to World War I, the armory was occupied by Companies A, C, and H, Second Infantry; Company G, Ninth Infantry; Battery B, First Field Artillery; and all of the Massachusetts Militia or National Guard.

Art Museum, Worcester, Mass. *Lois*

The Worcester Art Museum was born out of a meeting held at the home of Stephen Salisbury on February 25, 1896. Mr. Salisbury donated an acre of land and a fund of $100,000—half for construction of a building and the rest to be an endowment fund. The new museum on Salisbury Street was opened on May 10, 1898.

Fairlawn Hospital Worcester, Mass.

Fairlawn Hospital, founded in 1922, is located in the former residence of James Norcross, one of the founders of Norcross Brothers Company, Builders. Hospital wings have been added to the residence. James A. Norcross designed and built his residence in 1893.

The Cummings Block, located at 53, 55, and 57 Main Street opposite Court House Hill in 1911, housed Station A of the United States Post Office. The upper floors of the building were apartments.

The Graphic Arts Building is located on the corner of Foster and Commercial Streets. It was the first of its kind to be erected in the business district of the city. The building was constructed entirely of reinforced concrete and glass. It was ready for occupancy at the beginning of 1913.

The Greendale Village Improvement Society was located at 480 West Boylston Street on the corner of Brooks Avenue. Its charter was approved by the Massachusetts State Legislature on April 10, 1897. The society was concerned with the general welfare of the citizens of Greendale. It planted trees, collected rubbish, plowed snow, and provided fire protection.

The Home for Aged Men was located at 1199 Main Street in an estate that was donated by Isaac Curtis. It was incorporated in 1874. In November 1891, the home was opened for residents.

Isaiah Thomas began living in the house in 1775. It was located behind the courthouse near Lincoln Square. He was a printer, publisher, bookseller, and postmaster of Worcester. He published the *Massachusetts Spy*.

The Knights of Pythias Building was located at 114 Main Street at the end of Court House Hill. It was the former home of Francis H. Dewey, president of the Worcester Consolidated Street Railway Company The Worcester Knights of Pythias Charitable and Educational Association was organized June 30, 1914. On August 13, 1914, they took over the property at 114 Main Street. The three-story building had halls on the second and third floors. The ladies parlor and directors room was on the second floor, and the billiard, card, and reading rooms were on the street floor.

MANSION HOUSE, GREEN HILL PARK.   WORCESTER, MASS.

The mansion house at Green Hill Park, c. 1915, was rented by the park's commissioners for social occasions. A 1915 report indicated that between October 1914 and March 1915, the mansion was used eighty-one evenings for parties, which were attended by a total of 2,682 people.

The Masonic Temple located on Mower (Ionic) Avenue between Main and Beacon Streets was dedicated on September 3, 1914. Starting in 1867 the Worcester Masonic Charity and Educational Association had met at the old Post Office Building on Pearl Street. In 1914 the association was composed of 33 members, consisting of 3 representatives from each of the 11 Masonic bodies of Worcester.

The Hotel Borden was torn down to make way for the construction of the Medical Arts Building at 36 Pleasant Street. The building was completed about 1925. As the name implies, floors two through ten of the building contained physician's offices. A pharmacy occupied the first floor.

The building of the Worcester National History Society at 12 State Street was a bequest from the estate of the late Edward Conant in 1891. The object of the society is to instill a love of natural history in the minds of Worcester's youth.

OLD LADIES HOME
WORCESTER, MASS.

The Home for Aged Women was founded by Ichabod Washburn, a prominent manufacturer and philanthropist. He left a substantial portion of his estate toward its endowment. The home pictured here at 1183 Main Street was occupied on May 21, 1896.

The Osgood Bradley Building is located at the corner of Grafton and Franklin Streets. The building was constructed in 1916. The site is that of the old Bradley Car Works. The structure is eight stories high. A siding from the Boston and Albany Railroad, permanently erected in concrete, runs directly into the property at the third-floor level.

CHAPTER HOUSE D. A. R.   *The* OAKS

Col. Timothy Bigelow Chapter D. A. R.   *Worcefter, Maffachufettf*

The Timothy Paine House is located at 140 Lincoln Street. The house, known as The Oaks, was built by Tory Judge Timothy Paine prior to the Revolutionary War. It was owned by the Paine family until 1914, when it was sold to the Daughters of the American Revolution.

The Odd Fellows Building at 674 Main Street was dedicated on November 8, 1906. The building was arranged with various lodge rooms, anterooms, and large halls—all for the use of the city's Odd Fellows.

Lynch's Pleasant Street Theater is located at 17 Pleasant Street. Shown here are the main entrance, orchestra and stage, lobby, and ladies' room. When built in 1890, the theater was known as Lothrop's Opera House.

Poli's Theatre, Worcester, Mass.

Here is the interior of Poli's Theater, located at 28 Front Street. It was owned by Sylvester Z. Poli, who owned a similar theater in Springfield, Massachusetts. Poli later owned the Elm Street Poli Theater and the Franklin Square Theater. The theaters were sometimes used by stock companies, sometimes as vaudeville houses, and sometimes for motion pictures.

RESTAURARE INSTITUTE, 15 OREAD STREET, WORCESTER, MASS.

The Restaurare Institute was located at 15 Oread Street c. 1916. It lead the world in the treatment of alcoholism and drug diseases. Alcoholics were sobered in 30 minutes, their craving destroyed instantly without sickness. The institute was operated by physicians J.H. and E.B. Brownell.

Shown here is the South Worcester Branch Library. Samuel S. Green, after 38 years as the city's head librarian, resigned in 1909. The opening of branch libraries had been suggested by him in the past. Ex-Mayor James Logan was responsible for securing a gift of $75,000 from Andrew Carnegie to build three such branch libraries. Three cornerstones were laid on March 27, 1913—one at Greendale, one at Quinsigamond, and one at South Worcester. The libraries were opened in February 1914.

The exchange of the New England Telephone Company was located on the corner of Mechanic and Norwich Streets. The telephone company moved into the building on June 20, 1896. At that time there were 1,376 subscribers; in 1906 there were 9,289; and in 1914 there were 15,000.

Located at 184 Main Street at the corner of George Street is the Thule Music Hall Association Building. It was erected in 1905 by the Swedish citizens of the city and contained the Thule, Svea, and Continental Halls—the finest of their kind for lodges, concerts, balls, fairs, and banquets.

The Woman's Club Building is located on the corner of Salisbury and Tuckerman Streets. The club was the most exclusive women's organization in the city. It was organized in December 1880.

Tuckerman Hall is located in the Woman Club's Building. The building was constructed c. 1902 on land given to the club by Stephen Salisbury.

The Worcester County Jail was located on Summer Street. The first County House of Correction was erected in 1819. In 1832 40 cells were installed. In 1873 the building was completely renovated. It was relocated in the 1960s to Boylston to make way for a new post office.

The YMCA Building, located at 10 Elm Street, extended the entire block with a second entrance on Pearl Street. Constructed in 1887, it contained one of the finest gymnasiums in the country. The building was 154 feet long, 58 feet at its widest point, and cost $150,000 to complete and furnish.

Six

Religion

The Dewey Street Baptist Church, pictured here *c.* 1910, was located at 305 Park Avenue. The church was founded in 1872 in a chapel that was built on Dewey Street. The new meetinghouse on Park Avenue was first used for services on Thanksgiving Day in 1886.

The Massachusetts Christian Endeavor Union held its 1906 convention from October 25–28. Conventionaires posed on the steps of city hall for this picture. The First Baptist Church was the headquarters for the convention. The Young People's Society of Christian Endeavor was founded February 2, 1881. It is nonsectarian, but confined chiefly to the Congregational, Baptist, and other Protestant churches.

The First Church of Christ Scientist held its city meetings at the Woman's Club until 1913. The building shown here on Main Street, near Oberlin Street, was opened in 1913.

The First Church of Christ Disciples was founded in 1860. This church, located on 829 Main Street at the corner of Benefit Street, was dedicated on September 12, 1886.

The Inasmuch Club of the Highland Street Church of Christ was organized on September 22, 1908. The work of the club was to help the church, aid the needy, and to look after sick people and shut-ins.

The Greendale People's (Independent Congregational) Church, pictured here in Greendale c. 1910, was founded in 1895. Its actual location was on Francis Street at the corner of Bradley Avenue.

The Union Church, located on Chestnut Street opposite Pearl Street, was founded in 1836. This church was constructed by the Webb Granite and Construction Company of Worcester in 1898. A popular fair called "The Marketplace" was held by the Woman's Association of the Church in 1910.

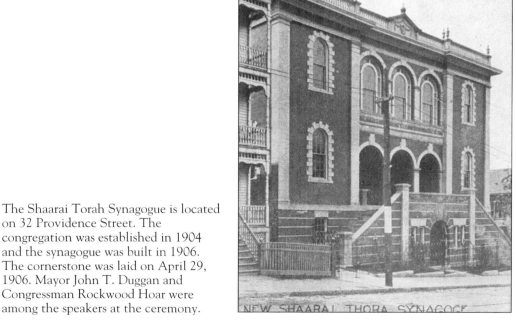

The Shaarai Torah Synagogue is located on 32 Providence Street. The congregation was established in 1904 and the synagogue was built in 1906. The cornerstone was laid on April 29, 1906. Mayor John T. Duggan and Congressman Rockwood Hoar were among the speakers at the ceremony.

The Swedish Evangelical Lutheran Gethsemane Church, shown here c. 1906, was located on Mulberry Street near Prospect Street. Incorporated in 1881, it was known as the First Lutheran Church. In 1911 the congregation moved to a new church at Belmont and Orchard Streets.

The Trinity Evangelical Lutheran Church was built at the corner of Lancaster and Salisbury Streets in 1952. Three Lutheran parishes were consolidated. They were the Swedish Evangelical Lutheran Gethsemane Church, the Swedish Finnish Evangelical Lutheran Church, and the Calvary Lutheran Church.

The Trinity Methodist Episcopal Church was located on the corner of Chandler and Main Streets. It was the successor to the first Methodist church in the city. The church building was constructed in 1871 and could probably seat more worshippers than any other Protestant church in the city. It was torn down in 1929 to make way for the widening of Chandler Street.

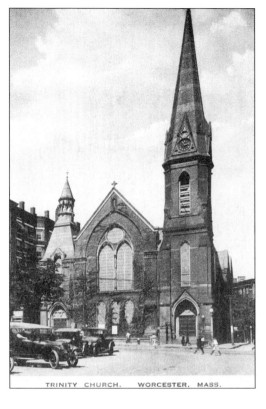

TRINITY CHURCH.   WORCESTER, MASS.

THE FIRST PRESBYTERIAN CHURCH.
MAIN AND HERMON STREETS
WORCESTER, MASS.

The First Presbyterian Church, located on the corner of Main and Hermon Streets, pictured here c. 1910, was founded in 1886. Its present location was formerly occupied by the Main Street Baptist Church.

83

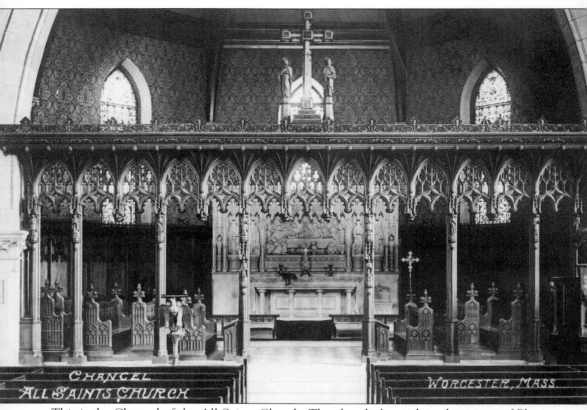

This is the Chancel of the All Saints Church. The church, located on the corner of Pleasant and Irving Streets, was dedicated in 1877. It was built using Longmeadow Brownstone. Both the church and its chapel contain organs.

St. John's Church, originally called Christ's Church, is located on Temple Street. It was the first Catholic church in central or western Massachusetts, and is the mother parish of two dioceses: Springfield and Worcester. This church was constructed in 1845.

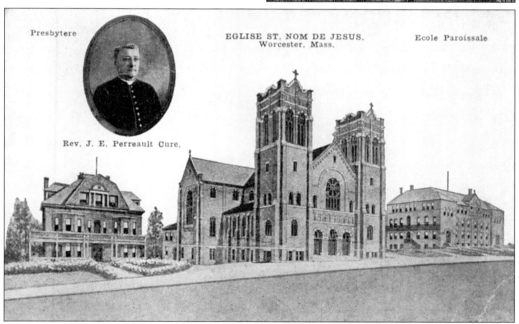

The Church of the Holy Name of Jesus is located on Illinois Street. It was built to serve the French Roman Catholics in the southern part of the city. Work on the church began in 1895 when a basement place of worship was built, and the church was occupied in 1896. Work on the church continued in stages until it was dedicated on December 24, 1916. The rectory was built in 1896 and the parish school in 1898.

MAIN ALTER
St. Casimir's Lithuanian R. C. Church

This is the main altar of St. Casimer's Lithuanian Roman Catholic Church—the first Lithuanian church in the city. The cornerstone of the church, located on the corner of Providence and Waverly Streets, was blessed on May 31, 1903, and six months later the first services were held in the basement. The church was blessed on October 12, 1916.

WNĘTRZE KOŚCIOŁA M. B. CZĘSTOCHOWSKIEJ W WORCESTER, MASS.

INTERIOR OF ST. MARY'S POLISH R. C. CHURCH, WORCESTER, MASS.

This is the interior of St. Mary's Polish Roman Catholic Church. The church, located at 5 Richland Street, was founded in 1904 and serves the city's Polish community.

ÉCOLE ST. JOSEPH, WORCESTER, MASS.

St. Joseph's Grammar School was located at 81 Plantation Street. It was one of the many schools in the Catholic parochial school system. The first parochial school was in the first Catholic parish. It was named St. John's School for Girls and was opened in 1872. In the 1950s the system contained 52 elementary and 16 secondary schools.

The AOH Hall was located at 26 Trumbull Street. The Ancient Order of Hibernians, a Catholic-Irish Society, was established in 1863 to assist Irish Immigrants. Located at street level is the Athy Funeral Home.

Worcester, Mass., Sisters of Notre Dame Home.

The Sisters of Notre Dame De Namur maintain a residence and convent at 555 Plantation Street, which overlooks the north end of Lake Quinsigamond. It was constructed in 1900 by McDermott Brothers, general building contractors.

The First Unitarian Church located at 90 Main Street on Courthouse Hill was founded in 1785. The church was severely damaged by the hurricane in 1938. This picture was taken after the church was rebuilt.

The Second Advent Christian Church, located at the corner of Chandler and Piedmont Streets, was founded in 1842. The Second Advent movement in the city was made in anticipation of the predicted end of the world on February 15, 1843. After the fatal day had passed, a formal organization of the Adventists took place.

First Universalist Church, 62 Pleasant St., Worcester, Mass

Handcolored

The First Universalist Church, located at 62 Pleasant Street, was founded in 1841. The first house of worship was located at the corner of Main and Foster Streets until the new church on Pleasant was occupied in 1871.

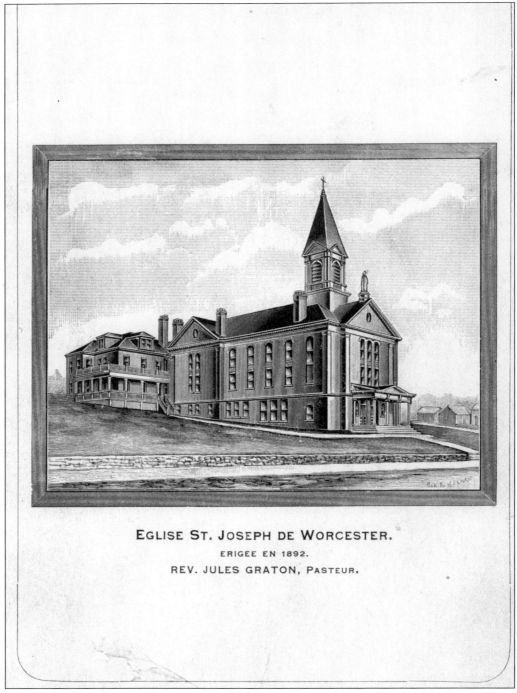

EGLISE ST. JOSEPH DE WORCESTER.

ERIGEE EN 1892.

REV. JULES GRATON, PASTEUR.

St. Joseph's Church, erected in 1892, was built to serve French-Canadian Catholics in the city. In 1930, after moving to its new church on Hamilton Street, the congregation sold the church building to St. George's Syrian Orthodox Church. St. George's was organized in 1905 and was first located at 100 Wall Street. It relocated to 32 Wall Street in 1930.

90

Seven
Schools

The Adams Square School was one of seven schools built during the term of Mayor Samuel Winslow (1886–90). It was located on Burncoat Street opposite Millbrook Street. It served grades one to eight in 1915. There were 9 teachers and 312 pupils in the school.

The Belmont Street School, located on Belmont Street at the corner of Clayton Street, served grades one to eight in 1915. There were 19 teachers and 665 pupils.

Gates Lane was named after Simon Gates, an early settler in the city. The Gates Lane School, located at Gates Lane and Main Street near Webster Square, served grades kindergarten through eight in 1915. There were 15 teachers and 529 pupils.

The Greendale School, located on Leeds Street at the corner of Fairhaven Road, served grades kindergarten to eight. In 1915 there were 12 teachers and 403 pupils.

Lake View was a settlement west of Lake Quinsigamond and south of Belmont Street. A railroad station, schoolhouse, church, post office, and stores were all located there. The Lake View School was located on Lakeview Street. It served grades kindergarten to eight. In 1915 there were 7 teachers and 241 pupils.

The Midland Street School is one of the many schoolhouses built during the 1896–98 period. These schoolhouses provided accommodations for 2,800 pupils. Located on the corner of Midland and Huntley Streets near Newton Square, it served grades kindergarten to seven in 1915. There were 10 teachers and 331 pupils.

The first Providence Street School building was completed in 1865 at a cost of $10,743. Located on Providence Street at the corner of Grafton Street, it served grades kindergarten to seven in 1915. There were 21 teachers and 675 pupils.

The First Tatnuck School was built around 1860 and housed 56 pupils. As the city's population pushed westward, the Tatnuck School seen in this photo was constructed. Located on Pleasant Street opposite Willard Avenue, it served grades kindergarten to eight in 1915. There were 8 teachers and 247 pupils.

The Thomas Street School was built around 1851, during the term of Peter C. Bacon, the city's third mayor. Located on the corner of Thomas and Summer Streets, it served grades kindergarten to eight in 1915. There were 13 teachers and 434 pupils.

Pictured here are the manual arts teachers of the public schools. The poster in the window is dated May 16, which means this picture was probably taken during spring vacation in April, as they seem prepared for April's showers and cool weather. The picture was mailed on June 22, 1911, by Arthur A. Pelton, a manual training teacher, to Daniel Dyer. From left to right are three unidentified teachers, Ball (of the Manual Training School), Traill (Millbury Street School), Donaldson, Atkins (Dix Street School), Bean (director of the Manual Training School), an unidentified teacher, and Dyer (Belmont Street School).

English High School was located at the corner of Irving and Chatham Streets. When the curriculum of the high schools was changed at the end of the 1914 school year, the name of the school was changed to Classical, and the name of the school formerly known as Classical was changed to Commerce.

North High School was located on the corner of Salisbury and Lancaster Streets opposite the Worcester Art Museum. Occupied in 1915, it was the city's fourth high school.

On September 20, 1911, Girl's Trade School was opened in a leased building at 2 State Street. In less than three years the building was over-crowded. The city purchased land for a new building near the corner of Chatham and High Streets. David H. Fanning, president of Royal Worcester Corset Company, presented the sum of $100,000 to the city for use towards the erection of a new building. That new building was named the David Hale Fanning Trade School for Girls and was dedicated on December 20, 1921.

The Oread, Worcester, Mass.

The Oread was located on Goat's Hill at the end of Castle Street off of 800 Main Street. Eli Thayer, educated in Worcester at the Manuel Labor School and a graduate of Brown University, returned to Worcester to act as principal of Worcester Academy. While there, he was convinced that women should be given the advantages of pre-college, higher education. In 1851 he established the Oread School for Women.

Clark University was founded by Jonas Clark. He chose Worcester because of its central location among the colleges of the East. The charter of the university was granted by the legislature of Massachusetts in 1887.

The Clark University Freshmen were all wet at the university pond in 1914. They had lost the annual rope pull to the juniors. The message on the back of the picture says, "This is a picture of our annual rope pull. The juniors stand on one side of the pond and the freshmen stand on the other side, and the tug of war ensues. This year we, the juniors were fortunate enough to pull the freshmen through."

An aerial view shows the Worcester Polytechnic Institute. In the foreground is the intersection of Park Avenue and Institute Road. The campus of the school is in the upper right and the athletic field is in the center of the picture.

This is 6 Humbolt Avenue, the chapter house of Sigma Alpha Epsilon Fraternity at Worcester Polytechnic Institute, c. 1920. There were six other fraternities with chapter houses—Phi Gama Delta, Delta Tau, Alpha Tau Omega, Theta Chi, Lamda Chi Alpha, and Phi Sigma Kappa.

100

Gaskill Field is Worcester Academy's athletic grounds. The field house and grounds, located on Providence Street, were constructed and finished in 1910. The field was named in honor of Judge Francis A. Gaskill, the third president of the board of trustees. It contains two baseball fields, the football field, a quarter-mile track, three tennis courts, and the field house.

The freshmen of this 1907 Worcester Academy Football Squad would play their final season in a brand-new field. They played against the following teams in 1910: Morris Heights School, Springfield Training, Dartmouth freshmen, Wesleyan Academy, Cushing Academy, Harvard Freshmen, and Williston Academy. Their record was two wins, three losses, and two ties.

Miss Kimball's School for Girls was located on the corner of May and Woodland Streets. It offered college-preparatory courses and special courses for young ladies and girls. Superior advantages were had in music, art, languages, physical fitness, and voice culture.

Highland Military Academy, Worcester, Mass.

A. P. Lundborg, Worcester, Mass.   Handcolored

The Highland Military Academy, located on Salisbury Street, was founded by Caleb B. Metcalf in 1856. He was a teacher in Worcester's public schools for many years. This school was a boarding school and a large number of its pupils came from a distance. The school continued until 1912, when the property was sold for residential purposes.

AMERICAN SCHOOL OF MUSIC.

PIANOFORTE CLASS   JOHN FREDERICK DONNELLY, DIRECTOR.   WORCESTER, MASS.

The pianoforte class of the American School of Music poses for this picture with Director John F. Donnelly. In 1912 Mr. Donnelly was a music teacher with offices in the Taylor Building at 476 Main Street.

The Domestic Training Institute, shown here c. 1910, was located at 158 Institute Road at the home of Mrs. Frank M. Wethered. She was a former teacher at the School of Domestic Science, which was located at the Oread Castle. When owner Henry D. Perky passed away, several of the students approached Mrs. Wethered to continue their studies. She agreed to help and the Worcester Domestic Science School was born. The school occupied several buildings on Institute Road and Dean Street.

A CORNER OF THE SCHOOL ROOM

MASSACHUSETTS ENGINEERING SCHOOL

A Nursery of Intellectual Progress, under the personal direction of THOS. F. MYERS, the man who made more Engineers than any other man on earth. ::

THE FAMOUS MYERS SYSTEM

CLASSES DAY AND EVENING

OPEN THE YEAR ROUND

26 AUSTIN STREET
WORCESTER, MASS.

IT TAKES BUT A FEW WEEKS TO COMPLETE A COURSE

The Massachusetts School of Engineering was established in 1905. Thomas F. Meyers was the director of the school. He also established schools of engineering in Boston and Springfield. Students were trained for positions as stationary fireman and engineers. The school was often called upon to inspect the large steam and electric plants in the factories and mills of the city.

Eight

Events

The City of Worcester.
This card entitles the bearer to
admission to the new City Hall
at the Dedication Exercises
April 28th 1898 at Two o'clock P.M.

Compliments of

On April 23, 1894, the General Court passed an act to allow the city to borrow over its debt limit for the purpose of building a new city hall. On April 23, 1896, the contract for the construction of the building was awarded to Norcross Brothers. The cornerstone was laid on September 12, 1897, and the new city hall was dedicated on April 28, 1898. Although $650,000 was appropriated for the task, the final cost of the building and its furnishings was $23,031.23 less than that amount.

In spite of workers threatening to strike, the white city was expected to open for the season on May 20, 1905. Although actually located on the Shrewsbury side of Lake Quinsigamond, all references to the park indicated it was in Worcester. The Worcester Consolidated Street Railway played a large roll in the financing of the park.

10600 President Roosevelt at the Holy Cross Commencement, June 1905, Holy Cross College, Worcester, Mass.

President Theodore Roosevelt visited Worcester for the second time on June 21, 1905. He arrived at Union Station at 9:28 a.m. to the cheers of thousands. He proceeded to the commencement exercises at Clark College. After Clark's exercises he went to the graduation at Holy Cross College. He left Union Station at 2:30 p.m. for Washington.

Crowds gather at the courthouse for the unveiling of the equestrian statue of Major-General Charles Devens on July 4, 1906. General Devens, a lawyer with a degree from Harvard, served as city solicitor for three years prior to entering the military to lead troops in the Civil War. After the war he was named a judge in the Supreme Court of Massachusetts. He also served as attorney general of the United States during the administration of President Hayes. General Devens died on January 7, 1891, at the age of 71, after a brief illness.

Eagle's Hall on 11 Pleasant Street was decorated with flags and buntings in celebration of the 1906 state convention of the Massachusetts Association of the Fraternal Order of Eagles that took place on August 1–2. Delegates from 40 of the 52 aeries of the state participated in a parade that was reviewed by Governor Curtis Guild.

The circus came to town in 1906. The parade of elephants passes Gibbons Piano at 145 Main Street and Ballou's Paint Store at 143 Main Street on its way to Lincoln Square.

J. HESLOR & CO.'S EXHIBITION, "BEN HUR" FLOUR
Worcester Food Show, February 28 to March 9, 1907

The Worcester Food Show was held at Mechanics Hall from February 28 to March 9, 1907. A great showing of splendid exhibits, pretty young women daintily dressed in white and colors, sweet music, the aroma from a variety of foods, and attractive booths were the magnets drawing crowds to the food fair.

Members of the Worcester Yacht Club pose in front of their clubhouse on Indian Lake. The club was an organization of those who owned boats and canoes on Indian Lake.

Prince Wilhelm of Sweden visited Worcester on August 26, 1907. This arch on Front Street was constructed in his honor. Thousands of Swedish immigrants and their children gathered to greet him. After accepting a key to the city from Mayor John T. Duggan, the prince proceeded to Mechanics Hall to give an address expressing his thanks to the city for its hospitality.

The north side of city hall was the location for the dedication of the George Frisbie Hoar statue on June 26, 1908. The late senator was memorialized by the city after his death on September 30, 1904, with services at Mechanics Hall on Patriots Day, April 19, 1905. He was a resident of the city for more than 50 years.

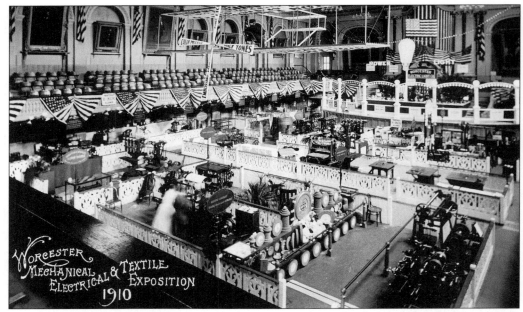

The Worcester Mechanical, Electrical, and Textile Exposition was held at Mechanics Hall from February 2–5, 1910. This is a view looking from the rear balcony towards the stage. One of the displays was a house of electricity in which only electrical devices were used for various things, from toasting bread to ironing clothes.

This is a view of the 1910 exposition looking from the balcony near the stage towards the rear. The exposition had 70 interesting and educational exhibits, some of which included chickens hatched by electricity, a demonstration of how envelopes were made, a new system of water pumping, an elastic stocking loom, and a Turkish towel loom.

The New England Corn Show was held at the fair grounds in Greendale from November 7–12, 1910. It was the first of its kind in New England. One of the displays, the bungalow of corn shown here, was shingled with ears of corn. On the roof was a Dutch windmill operation constructed using corn stalks. Draperies, found in each window, were made of corn kernels.

The events of the 1910 New England Fair were highlighted by aviator Frank W. Goodale and his airship. Mr. Goodale, only 21 years old, was expected to fly the airship to city hall, circle the clock tower, and sail back to the fair grounds.

FIFTH ANNUAL CONVENTION

[ASSOCIATED]

Y. M. H. A.'s AND Y. W. H. A.'s
OF · NEW · ENGLAND

WORCESTER · MASSACHUSETTS
SEPTEMBER 4TH, 5TH AND 6TH
NINETEEN HUNDRED AND FIFTEEN

The Convention of the Young Men's Hebrew Associations and the Young Women's Hebrew Associations of New England took place at the Bancroft Hotel. Large meetings also took place at Mechanics Hall. There was a field day that Monday at Boulevard Park.

These British soldiers, set up on the common c. 1916, were recruiting British citizens in the United States to join the war effort. Great Britain called up five million men to fight in the war during 1916 and 1917. The messages on the posters say, "Britishers Come Across Now," and, "Britishers Enlist Today."

The women of the Salvation Army "manned" this booth in front of city hall during the week of May 19–25, 1919. The National Salvation Army Fund Raising Drive began on May 19, 1919. Saturday, May 25, 1919, was declared "Donut Day." The women's committee handed out imitation donuts as tags to each person who donated to the army's home service fund. Real donuts were also sold.

The Victory Arch on the common was constructed by L. Rochford and Son General Contractors. Plaster was the material used for the job. The total height was 52 feet and the width was 40 feet. The opening of the arch was 20 feet wide and 32 feet high.

This arch was constructed on the common in April of 1919. It was built to honor all of Worcester's boys who enlisted in either the army or the navy for service in the war. The returning soldiers passed under the arch on May 1, 1919, during a big welcome-home parade.

Nine

Disasters

The deputy-chief engineer sits with his driver in front of the Fire Department Headquarters Building on the corner of Mercantile and Foster Streets, c. 1910. In 1911 the chief engineer was George S. Coleman and the deputy-chief engineer was Wesley N. Avery.

The Knowles Building on the left was in ruins as a result of the city's worst fire up to that time. It occurred at 3:00 a.m. on January 19, 1921. A night watchman for the adjacent S. Marcus Store discovered the fire around the elevator well on the first floor. Fortunately the wind was blowing from the northwest. Had the wind been blowing from the south, it was doubtful that the fire could have been prevented from going all the way through to Court House Hill.

Flames from the Knowles Building jumped across Main Street to the east side and destroyed the W.H. Sawyer block, partially destroyed the Willard Hardware block, the Monahans Sporting Goods Store, and the Williams Book Store. Fifteen small fires were set by sparks from the large fire.

118

This was the scene on Park (Franklin) Street, across from city hall, after a fire that started in Samuel Starkworth's Wallpaper Store at 10:30 p.m., October 14, 1908. An entire city block was razed, including Notre Dame Church.

A major fire in the Steven's block, on Southbridge Street across from the post office, occurred on February 8, 1906. Ten firemen were injured while fighting the four-alarm fire. It was one of the hardest-fought fires in years.

The Worcester Protective Department of Insurance Fire Patrol was stationed at Barton Place across from city hall. It was supported by the insurance companies doing business in Worcester for the protection of property from damage by fire and water. In 1911 the patrol consisted of nine members.

Three horses pull the men of Chemical Number Three. The city had three chemical companies in 1911. They were located at the stations on John Street, Foster Street, and Burncoat Street.

The men of Engine Number Two pose in front of their station house at 108 Beacon Street *c.* 1910. The city maintained seven engine companies in 1911. In addition to Beacon Street, the other companies were located at Mercantile Street, School Street, Pleasant Street, Webster Street, Bloomingdale Road, and Eastern Avenue.

This is the steamer part of Engine Two. In 1911 engineers of steamers were paid $3.10 per day.

The men of Hose Company Number Five are shown here *c.* 1910. In 1911 Worcester had eleven hose companies. They were stationed at Prescott Street, Grafton Street, Cambridge Street, Foster Street, Portland Street, Millbury Street, Lamartine Street, Providence Street, Woodland Street, West Boylston Street, and Mercantile Street.

Six men were assigned to Ladder Company Number Five in 1911. Ladder Number Five, shown here, was located at the 100 Providence Street Fire Station. There were five other ladder companies in the city. They were located at the stations on Portland Street, Prescott Street, Mercantile Street, Webster Street, and West Boylston Street.

56/911

Jan 23 — Box 262 at 10:43 a.m. Electricity from Finger Tips Started the Blaze Mrs John F. Kelleher wife of the manager of the new Park Hotel was using naphtha in Cleaning a light dress Sparks from finger tips lighted the garment It is the first Case on record in Worcester where a fire has been Caused by hand friction in the use of Naphtha the only loss was to the Dress Warren at Hose 4 Meacham at Chemical 3 Stone Hose 9

time — 1 Hour

" 23 — Box 5 at 6:54 Pm for a fire in the home of Mrs Margaret McConvill Courtney No. 112 Park Street Damage 200 Dollars Stone at Hose 4

time — 1 Hour

.. 24 — Box 12 at 10:67 a.m. for a fire in the Cellar of the House owned by John F. and Martha T Armstrong Damage Slight Capt William A Adams Ladder 3 was Injured by a Fall from his Truck in front of Headquarters Striken the left forward wheel and Sustaining a Compound fracture of the lower Jaw and a dislocation of the left Shoulder His name was placed on the Dangerous list at the City Hospital Tinn and Warren at hose 4

time — 1 Hour

" 24 — Box 481 at 1:34 Pm Grass fire no damage

" 25 — Box 61 at 8:55 a.m. for a fire in Waste Basket In the home of R B. Brown No 39 Highland St No Damage Warren Eng 1 Meacham at Hose 16 Stone at Engine 2

Each fire station maintained a daily log of the alarms it responded to. This is a page from the daily log of Engine Number Four stationed on Pleasant Street, dated January 23–25, 1911. One of the entries for January 23 reads, "Box 262 at 10:43 a.m. Electricity from finger tips started the blaze. Mrs. John F. Kelliher, wife of the manager of the new Park Hotel, was using Naphtha in cleaning a light dress. Sparks from finger tips lighted the garment. It is the first case on record in Worcester where a fire has been caused by hand friction in the use of Naphtha. The only loss was to the dress."

No 1 Barbers Crossing

A crowd gathers at the train wreck that occurred at Barber's Crossing, in the Greendale section of the city, at noon on October 2, 1907.

No 2 Barbers Crossing

BOSTON & MAINE

The wreck at Barber's Crossing was between a Boston and Maine freight train. The engineer of the passenger train failed to see the signal that told the passenger train to stop.

A crowd has gathered to view the wrecked cars from the Barber's Crossing wreck. Six people were injured in the wreck. The engines were reduced to scrap iron, and the freight and passenger cars became kindling wood.

People stand on the wrecked cars at Barber's Crossing. Wreckage can be seen blocking the tracks. On the right you can see the chimneys of the Norton Company.

Selected Bibliography

Blanchard, F.S. and Company. *Dictionary of Worcester and Vicinity.* 1889.

Carlson, Stephen and Thomas Harding. *Worcester Trolleys Remembered.* Worcester: Worcester Regional Transit Authority, 1985.

City of Worcester. *Memorial Services of George Frisbie Hoar.* Worcester: Blanchard Press, 1907.

Diocese of Worcester. *Official Reference and Information Guide.* 1915.

Drew Allis Company. *Worcester Directories 1892–1930.*

Eastus, Charles W. and John F. McClymer. *GA Til Amerika: The Swedish Creation of an Ethnic Identity for Worcester, Massachusetts.* Worcester: Worcester Historical Museum, 1994.

Farnsworth and O'Flynn. *The Story of Worcester Massachusetts.* Worcester: Davis Press, 1934.

Feingold, Norma. *Shaarai Torah: Life Cycle of a Synagogue.* Worcester: Worcester Historical Museum, 1991.

Frost, Jack. *The Church in Worcester, New England.* Hawthorne Press, 1956.

Knowlton, Elliot B. and Sandra Gibson-Quigley. *Worcester's Best* (2nd Edition). Worcester: Preservation Worcester, 1996.

Mange, Paul. *Our Inns From 1718–1918.*

Nutt, Charles. *History of Worcester and its People.* New York: Lewis Historical Publishing Company, 1919.

Park Commissioners. *Annual Report 1914–15.* Worcester: Commonwealth Press, 1915.

Rice, Franklin P. *The Worcester of Eighteen Hundred and Ninety-Eight.* Worcester: Blanchard and Company, 1899.

Trinity Lutheran Church. *Trinity Lutheran Church.* Worcester: Commonwealth Press, 1952.

Sandrof, Ivan. *Your Worcester Street.* Franklin Publishing, 1948.

Spears, John P. *Old Landmarks and Historic Spots.* Worcester: Commonwealth Press, 1931.

Tulloch, Donald. *Worcester City of Prosperity 1914.* Worcester: Commonwealth Press.

WPI. *The Aftermath 1923.* Heffernan Press.

Worcester Telegram. *Worcester Telegram* (1905 to 1920 editions).

Worcester Bank and Trust Company. *Some Historical Houses of Worcester.* Walton Printing and Advertising Company, 1919.

Worcester Board of Trade. *A Tribute to the Colombian Year.* Worcester: F.S. Blanchard and Company, 1893.

Worcester Board of Trade. *Worcester* Magazine.